Don't Sweat
The Small Stuff

Don't Sweat
The Small Stuff

Marie Frost

Illustrations—Joyce Thimsen

KEY PUBLISHERS, INC.
Wheaton, Illinois

CONTENTS

Part Two
Church Undoings

Part Three
'Round and 'Round

INTRODUCTION

People are funny, aren't we! Even Christians. One thing I've noticed that always amazes me is that most Christians can rise to the occasion when facing serious emergencies, but minor difficulties often put us flat on our faces! I've seen Christians draw upon God-given reservoirs of strength and self-possession in crises and move through the trials successfully and even victoriously. But these same people have practically "gone into orbit" over trivial and ordinary problems that are a part of everyday life.

There are many explanations for unbecoming and unchristian behavior, but when all have been heard we realize that we fail in the small tests because we forget to draw upon the spiritual resources that brought us through the big tests. Crises, large and small, are steps in life that move us forward or backward. If we will, we Christians can meet them all in the power of Christ's life.

I do not know who first put the following advice in John Doe's lingo, but it hits home: "Friend, don't sweat the small stuff." A lot of our griefs would wither and die if we didn't pour so much spiritual perspiration over them!

In these pages you may see yourself—not because real names are used, but because these experiences take place all the time all over the country. I hope you can laugh at these experiences and learn from them. For your family's and friends' sake, for God's glory, and for your own happiness, I pray you will choose not to "sweat the small stuff."

PART ONE

Mother and Child

SAFETY FIRST?

Four-year-old Brian wants to ride a two-wheeled bike. Eight-year-old Maureen wants to use Mother's electric sewing machine. Thirteen-year-old Mark wants to take a twenty-mile bike trip with his friends.

In each case, Mother's reaction is, "My child will be hurt—she's too young, he can't handle it." It is instinctive for her to feel this way; she must be concerned for her children's safety.

But Mother must also realize that her children are developing new abilities daily, and she must encourage, not hinder, their growth. She might take a lesson from watching the action on the local playground: the kids who come alone are usually having a great time, daring and accomplishing many difficult feats, while off to the side stands an immaculately dressed toddler clutching Mommy's hand, afraid to venture over to the lowest swing. Too much security can be false security!

11

If Brian wants to ride the two-wheeler, Mother can help him! She can show Maureen the proper way to operate the sewing machine and encourage her to try—under supervision. Mark can start his hiking adventures with a shorter ride accompanied by a trusted older brother or friend.

Once the child has shown that he is ready for a new activity, Mother can give her approval and send him on his way. Burdening the child with exaggerated fears of what *might* happen is small stuff! Encouraging him to try something challenging is what life is all about. The praying mother can commit her child's well-being to God—and grow with her children!

MORE THAN CLOTHES

Terry's reception at home was typically stormy. "How did you make such a shambles of your clothes? Did you play football in those good pants? Look at those knees—I can never fix that. And will you please at least tie your shoes! You don't have to be sloppy on top of being dirty."

Accustomed to such scoldings, Terry hardly heard even the first sentence. He hadn't found a satisfactory answer for his mother in all his previous attempts.

If only Terry's mother would stop measuring *her* reputation by *his* appearance, and let him wear sturdy, washable play clothes like his friends. In trying to make Terry into her own every-hair-in-place image, she was shattering his image of himself.

Terry needs a mother who sees past his clothes to the boy himself. That kind of love-sight would inspire something like: "Hey, looks like you really had a workout! I'll have to fix that knee before you wear those pants again."

VALUABLES

Tiny Cindy reached for the vase on the table.

"No, no!" screamed Mother. But the warning came too late and the vase lay broken before her.

"Bad Cindy to break Mother's vase," said Mother as she started to pick up the pieces.

Realizing she had reaped Mother's disapproval, Cindy tried to help her pick up some of the glass.

Once again Mother's angry voice shrilled: "Naughty baby—leave glass alone!" and the command was reinforced with a resounding slap on Cindy's outstretched hand.

Confused at being rebuffed for helping her mother, Cindy ran crying from the room.

Mother continued to pick up the broken glass, and suddenly the vase didn't seem so valuable as she thought of Cindy. It really was small stuff in comparison with her daughter's happiness. Mother had some mending to do—of Cindy's hurt.

INTERIOR DEVASTATION

Mrs. Jordan viewed her eight-year-old daughter's room with dismay. The bedspread was crooked on the bed, the blanket beneath it was half on the floor. And wasn't there a less conspicuous place for those dolls with matted hair and missing limbs!

Suddenly startled by the sight of her frown in the mirror, Mrs. Jordan sighed and smiled wryly. She had once decided that her family's needs would always come before her own desires to have a tidy house. Perfect order was small stuff compared to a home that was enjoyed by its inhabitants!

LONG APRON STRINGS!

Benny is nine years old, but it's hard to tell. He sticks close to his mother, whines when he wants something, and begs his mother to read to him every night at bedtime. When things don't go his way, he generates a tantrum.

And why is Benny "socially retarded"? Frankly, his parents haven't helped him to grow up. If they don't remedy things, Benny may be permanently handicapped in his relationships with others. What to do?

Benny's whines should receive no response. A whine is normal for dogs, but not for humans, and Benny can be taught that only pleasant, intelligent expressions receive attention from parents.

Reading together is a profitable experience, but reading alone is also valuable and necessary. Benny must explore some new reading worlds by himself.

Tantrums must never be rewarded by acquiescence

to demands. When they don't produce results, Benny will give up the effort.

Of course, Benny may sulk. He may even increase his dependent behavior in the hope his parents will respond to his helplessness. But it won't last if Mother and Dad follow through with the new program. Simply put, the new regime assures that infantile actions will cause curtailment of privileges that are reserved for children who can handle them; and actions showing progress will be warmly approved and supported.

In time, Benny will learn that nine-year-olds can be as lovable as four-year-olds—on a much more satisfying level. Small stuff is only for small people!

CHIPPER'S CONTRIBUTION

Sarah's parakeet, Chipper, is something less than a delight to Sarah's mother. Chipper's cage is almost always surrounded by scattered bird seed to be picked up. The black family cat, doing what comes naturally, steadily shreds the curtains which he climbs in the hope of reaching Chipper. Mother feels guilty about hurting Sarah if she were to give the bird away, but she feels tense from suppressed irritation at having to take care of Chipper.

So much strain over one small bird! Mother could avoid most of the frustration by accepting the fact that Chipper is important to Sarah at this point in her life, and is therefore worth the toil required to care for the pet.

Sarah can help, of course. In fact, she will not benefit as she should from having a pet if she is not taught to care for Chipper cheerfully. God's eye is on the parakeet—and on people who care for it.

FOUL BALL

It was Little League season—or baseball blitz. "Volunteer" managers had been dragged from their armchairs into action, and sometimes the only ones happy about the situation were the players whose fathers bossed the teams!

Billy, whose father wasn't a manager, was probably the best pitcher on the Cardinals team. But did Billy pitch? No, not even in practice, because the manager's son, Jerry, wants to be a pitcher, and he needs all the practice he can get!

Billy doesn't appreciate this state of affairs, and neither does his father. So what should they do? Yell gibes from the bleachers? Stir discontent in other team members? Quit? Small stuff!

Billy's skill won't disappear this season if he doesn't pitch a lot. His career doesn't depend on this one year. There are other positions on the team, and Billy's ability will be noticed.

Besides, more than baseball is at stake—things like learning cooperation with others and giving one's best under difficult circumstances. Billy might even grow to be a better man by *not* "doing his thing." Play ball!

"REJECTED" CHILD

Nancy insisted that she should drive the car to school, and Mother countered with the reminder that the school bus went right past the house.

"You let Bill drive to school when he was my age," Nancy said accusingly.

"We-el-ll-ll-ll," said Mother, stalling for time to develop a good answer. She hated to say that Bill had been more responsible, but he was. Of course, the bus hadn't fit his busy schedule, either. But what if Nancy thought her mother was playing favorites!

Poor Mother! She's in a dilemma—of her own making! She's afraid of her own daughter! And she's fearful of her own ability to think through decisions.

Mother has forgotten that she's far ahead of her daughter in experience, and that God gave Nancy to her for training.

And if Nancy saw that her mother sympathized with her desire, there would be no real feelings of rejection. No need to sweat that small stuff!

"YOUR TURN!"

Listen to Joan and Patrick decide whose turn it is to wash the dishes:

"It's your turn because it's Wednesday."

"No, it's your turn because I did it for you last Tuesday."

"But what about the time I took your turn when you had to play in Little League?"

"Oh, I took care of that when you had your piano recital. Remember, Mother?"

And what is Mother doing? Sagging limply to the couch? Joining the shouting match? Snapping: "Never mind, I'll do it myself," in a martyr's tone?

Not if she's learned to ignore the small stuff!

Mother realizes that some bickering is inevitable. Observation has taught her that Joan's appeal for her mother's support is usually self-centered, and a case as tangled as this would confuse the FBI.

Accordingly, Mother deftly sidesteps the debate

and leaves the scene with the parting admonition: "Just don't leave till the job is done!" That strategy might accelerate the work and stifle the clamor simultaneously.

Getting the dishes done is small stuff when measured against Joan's and Patrick's need to go the "second mile" for each other. Which means that Mother may have to go the "third" or "fourth mile," but she remembers what her Companion said: "I will never leave you."

WHO'S IN CHARGE?

Jeannie, 13, has learned to intimidate her parents. When they wanted her to go out to dinner with the family, Jeannie insisted that faded jeans were good enough to wear. Her mother would not allow Jeannie to wear this outfit, but Jeannie remained adamant and the whole family stayed home.

How did a thirteen-year-old get control of the family? It wasn't hard—for Jeannie and the other clever children like her. They gradually take more and more control as the parents let control slip through their fingers. Perhaps the parents are lax in discipline, mistakenly thinking permissiveness is kindness. Or they may have forgotten the God-ordained authority of parent over child is far different from a buddy-buddy relationship.

Jeannie is still a child, and she's acting like one. But after all these years of self-assertiveness, she's a determined child.

The situation calls for a concerted campaign by both parents. Jeannie needs to be approached in a spirit of firm helpfulness and led to see her responsibility to other members of the family. The long-range battle should be won through small but steady advances as everyone "wins" and no worthy principle is sacrificed to "keep peace."

Going to the restaurant without Jeannie might have been the first step toward showing her that others will be considered equally with her. Faced with that consequence, her determined choice of unsuitable clothes might show up as the small stuff it really was.

"In honor preferring one another" . . . is as much for teen-aged Jeannies as for God-honoring parents!

SCORNED WISDOM

"But, Mother, I'd rather do it myself!"

Chuck did not smile politely as he spoke, and the words were like a knife to Mrs. Johnson. The place, his room; the subject, a poster for a citywide art contest. Mother, an artist herself, wanted to say, "Add a color here; subtract a line there." After all, she was the expert. But Chuck was having none of it.

And despite his refusing her advice—maybe *because* of it, she had to admit—his poster turned out beautiful. In fact, it won first prize—private art lessons from some well-known artists in the area.

In the subsequent lessons, Mrs. Johnson was astounded to see that the suggestions she had been making unsuccessfully to Chuck were now being accepted gladly from another source!

All parents have this experience at one time or another. And how hurt—or baffled—we are to see someone else take our place as counselor to our children. We may even wish for our child's failure to prove that we have been right!

But children need to grow up—and parents do too! Let's not sweat the small stuff of requiring recognition of our "wisdom." Let's assist as much as we can, and wisely lengthen the apron strings until they gradually vanish.

Will our children always resist our ideas and reject our values?

Not if they know the same Source of true knowledge and power that we do: the Master Teacher, Friend, and Savior. If you have introduced your children to the One who said, "Learn of Me," they'll grow more and more as you have grown.

"I will instruct (says the Lord) and guide you along the best pathway for your life; I will advise you and watch your progress" (Psalm 32:8, LB).

DECORATING DILEMMA

Sally's room needed redecorating. Her mother, a gentle, gracious woman, suggested a pale green with rose accents. To her astonishment, Sally wanted a room decorated mod style in red, white, and blue!

The idea was ghastly to Sally's mother, but she decided a sixteen-year-old was old enough to choose her own decor. She tried not to gasp audibly when she learned Sally was planning to paint one wall with red and white stripes and stars for accent!

Wild? Yes, in appearance. But it was hard to find anything morally questionable about Sally's taste in colors. And there was a good chance her taste would change before many months or years passed. If the dazzling sight hurt her eyes, Sally's mother could easily close the door.

When she thought about it, Sally's mother realized she was more concerned about the "big stuff" of agreeing on important things and keeping the lines of communication open with her daughter.

SWALLOWING PRIDE

"But, Johnny!" Mrs. Edgars pleaded. "If your grades don't improve, you're never going to make it to college. In fact, you may not make it through high school!"

Mrs. Edgars was not only concerned; she was desperate. College was the accepted way of life in the Edgars family. Both she and Dr. Edgars were distinguished college professors, and Johnny's four older brothers all had brilliant academic records.

"Where have we failed you?" moaned his mother. "Well, you just have to try harder. We'll get you a tutor. You're going to college if it kills us all."

Mrs. Edgars tried to ignore her son's slumped shoulders and the tears of anguish in his eyes. After all, she knew what was best for her son.

But the day that Johnny's principal politely but firmly told her that Johnny was not going to graduate with his class—in fact, might not graduate from high school at all—Mrs. Edgars' fierce pride crumpled.

47

She stood at the kitchen sink, fighting back tears as she prepared supper. Johnny, as usual, sat on the stool beside her, his fingers twisting nervously. He had never been in any trouble; he had always been the gentle "Mother's boy," spending time in the kitchen instead of pounding textbooks or rival athletes in sports.

"Johnny," she began falteringly, "your principal says you are not going to graduate this year. So you are not going to college next year, maybe never. Johnny, what do you really want out of life? What does it take to interest you in something?"

"Why, Mother," he replied, "don't you know? What I want most of all is to learn to cook just like you!"

It was a lightning bolt—and a glimmer of hope. The Edgars swallowed their pride and enrolled Johnny in a professional cooking school where he became an outstanding trainee. In time, the student who disgraced his parents became one of the top chefs in this country, known not only for his skill but for his exciting innovations.

The world is full of "Johnnys"—children that parents try to force into a conventional mold, when God has given them distinctive talents, dreams, inspirations.

"Don't sweat the small stuff." Most great men of the world were once considered embarrassingly "abnormal." Parents should rejoice over the differences among their children; God made each one marvelously unique, and to be ashamed of their differences is to be blind to His marvelous wisdom.

"Everything is appropriate in its own time. But though God has planted eternity in the hearts of man, even so, man cannot see the whole scope of God's work from beginning to end" (Ecclesiastes 3:11, LB).

PART TWO

Church
Undoings

WHO BRINGS THE FLOWERS?

Mrs. Shaw had brought flowers from her garden to decorate the church altar for the past ten years, in addition to teaching Sunday school and leading the missionary society. She had been proud of her efforts, and appreciative parishioners often spoke of her diligence.

Then one Sunday Mrs. James, who owned a greenhouse, also brought flowers. She was a new member of the congregation but was quite aware of Mrs. Shaw's regular donations. Her bouquets were larger and more beautiful. At first her lovely creations were put at the back of the church, then people began asking why they weren't at the front for greater enjoyment.

Mrs. Shaw took her problem to the church board. She wanted to know "just who is responsible for bringing flowers," assuming that she would be named. But the board decided that one thing Mrs. James could do well would be to bring flowers, so they officially gave her the job.

Mrs. Shaw thought of all those years she had unfailingly beautified the Lord's house, only to be rejected when someone with a greenhouse came along.

While Mrs. Shaw nursed her wounded feelings and Mrs. James gloried in her new recognition, the board members congratulated themselves on their promising newcomer and congregational members revelled in the fragrance and beauty of the sanctuary.

The smell rising from that church to heaven, however, was very unpleasant indeed; it was tinged with decay and death. Pride and preference are not small stuff, though strife over supplying flowers is. The Lord's response is: "There is no use now in burning sweet incense from Sheba before me. Keep your expensive perfumes! I cannot accept your offerings; they have no sweet fragrance for me." "Obey me and I will be your God and you shall be my people" (Jeremiah 6:20; 7:23, LB).

"THANK YOU, FAITHFUL SERVANT"

The climax for the vacation Bible school was program night, and all was in readiness for the performances of the various departments. It turned out to be an excellent program, and the Sunday school leaders thanked those who had worked diligently to make the project a success.

"Thank you's" were given to Mrs. Blake, who had charge of the snack program; Mrs. Neeley, transportation chairman; the departmental superintendents; the teachers; the pianists; teaching assistants; and even the ushers. Everyone was individually mentioned—except Miss Franklin. She was far in the background: all she did was fill in wherever there was a vacancy and take care of jobs other people forgot to do!

But how fortunate that hers was the name omitted. Miss Franklin was not looking for praise; she was serving "unto the Lord," and she remembered that God kept the records that counted!

Did she miss being commended publicly? Yes, she was human. But it was "small stuff" to grieve over an unintentional slight. "Each of us will be rewarded for his own hard work"—by the Lord himself! (1 Corinthians 3:8, LB)

THE PURLOINED CHAIR

Ten chairs were carefully arranged in a semicircle waiting to be used by Miss Esther's ten Junior pupils. While she went to get a flannelboard, Mr. Ryan took one of the chairs because he needed an extra one in the choir.

Miss Esther became so disturbed when she discovered the "theft" that she could hardly gain enough poise to begin the class. Billy didn't have his chair to sit on, and that missing detail disrupted the whole teaching plan!

The pupils observed Miss Esther's lack of control and promptly followed her example. Eventually the commotion reached the ears of Mr. Ryan, who guiltily returned the chair, though he had no idea it would cause trouble.

Miss Esther was a perfectionist in a very imperfect world. No matter how hard she tried to get everything in place, someone marred her plans. Sometimes she wondered if she shouldn't give up everything!

What a shame that Miss Esther's lesson that day was on the fruit of the Spirit: love, kindness, gentleness. . . . They got buried under a pile of "small stuff"—almost as if the teacher had memorized the lesson to say it but not live it!

CHANGE—ME?

The church has been having its Sunday evening service at 7 P.M. for twenty years. Everyone had been happy about the arrangement—at least Mr. Mayfield thought so until the youth director mentioned to a number of people that a change to six o'clock would aid the young people's group.

"Aha!" thought Mr. Mayfield. "A revolution is brewing . . . the old way is bad . . . they'll want to close the evening service next . . . all for some young people who want more time to play. It's liberalism, heresy!"

Dark suspicion—what fantasies it can contrive! Before pushing the panic button, Mr. Mayfield should seek the reason for the proposed change. The explanation is that the youth group finds its six o'clock meeting ended too abruptly by the seven o'clock service. And they have more time to meet in the evening than earlier in the afternoon.

65

Did Mr. Mayfield trust the youth director? Were he and other tradition-bound saints willing to change things to help fellow-saints? It's strictly small stuff—until someone blows it up to threatening proportions and forces an explosion that might hurt a lot of people.

GENEROUS ADVISORS

The new church building was almost finished. Since the congregation is small and finances have dwindled, the group decided to paint the inside of the building themselves. Enthusiasm brought out many helpers at first, but as time went on only a faithful few returned regularly to work.

Among the tireless ones was a lady who consistently gave of her self. One of her little jobs was to fill nail holes in the window frames—eyesores a novice painter did not bother to take care of.

She pressed putty into the holes with her fingers until someone came along and suggested: "Why not use a razor blade? It works better." So Mrs. Adams used a razor blade, but it didn't work better for her, and then another workman suggested using a putty knife.

Mrs. Adams worked doggedly with the putty knife

though it was obviously too large for the job. Another gentleman wandered by and offered a yellow putty stick to fill the holes. With a brief trial, Mrs. Adams saw that the shade of the putty stick didn't match the paint. At that point she quietly retreated from the scene, muttering to herself: "Let the men do it, since they know so much about it!"

But as she contemplated the situation, Mrs. Adams didn't feel comfortable at all. She realized that church fellowships have been ruptured by such small stuff as this. She guessed the men were *trying* to be helpful.

Early the next morning Mrs. Adams went to church alone and filled the holes with the putty stick. Then she repainted the window frames with a second coat of matching paint. The frames needed more paint anyway.

When the men complimented Mrs. Adams on the result, she prudently omitted explaining the details that might embarrass her advisors. She had learned not to sweat the small stuff. God asks her to live peaceably with others—even men who know more about building a church than a woman does!

CUPBOARD CALAMITY

The church secretary kept her supply cupboard in the pastor's office. It seemed to be the safest place and the pastor was generous about sharing the office space.

When the youth group needed a place to meet and there seemed to be no available room, the pastor suggested that they use his office. Since the group was large, the accommodating pastor moved the secretary's cupboard into the adjoining hall.

The following Sunday after the secretary found her cupboard in the hall, she appeared to be suffering from apoplexy—stumbling woodenly around the church and rejecting all attention from concerned inquirers. Irrationally, but truly, she felt she had been pushed aside along with her cupboard.

The pastor thought it was small stuff to be so upset by an action for others, so he felt an apology was silly, though he did give an explanation.

Does God's Word say anything about this situation? Yes: "If you are . . . offering a sacrifice to God, and suddenly remember that a friend has something against you . . . go and apologize and be reconciled to him, and then come and offer your sacrifice to God" (Matt. 5:23, 24 LB). The pastor did know God's Word, and to have a clear conscience toward God and men, he had to make the apology—which he did. He also moved the cupboard back into the office, and once again tranquility reigned.

No command of Scripture—nor any human hurt—can be lightly regarded if God's blessing is to rest on his people.

VAIN IMAGININGS

The Sunday school hour was in progress and Miss Cabot carried forth with pride and confidence in her corner of the room. Her lesson was well-prepared, and she had made flannelgraph figures to illustrate the Bible story. It seemed a perfect situation until the Sunday school superintendent slipped quietly into the back row to observe.

Miss Cabot became flustered and her mind muttered protests while her mouth meandered through the Bible story. "What on earth is the super-intendent doing here ... doesn't he think I know how to teach ... I've been teaching over thirty years ... I should think I know a few things ... who else could he find that would put so much effort into teaching this class ... just last week I took my class into the city to visit the museum ... you knock your-self out and no one even notices ... the more you do the more people criticize."

If only Miss Cabot had quieted her wild imaginings and gone on with the lesson, everyone would have profited. The superintendent was not out to "get" Miss Cabot; after the class he told Miss Cabot how much he appreciated her teaching. Even that encouragement failed to dispel her ruffled feelings at having someone check up on her. Was she overconfident, or actually fearful?

"Don't be conceited, sure of your own wisdom. Instead, trust and reverence the Lord" (Proverbs 3:7, 8, LB).

BACH, ROCK—AND *POP*!

It wasn't the words of the song but the beat of the new music that bothered Mr. Hale. He had been a faithful member of the church choir for a long time, and he actually preferred classical music as to form. He tolerated lively "gospel singing," but he was not about to succumb to syncopated, so-called "religious" songs. He approached the choir director with his convictions when the "new sound" became unbearable.

The choir director didn't share Mr. Hale's feelings about one kind of music. He liked to try new styles when the words carried a message. He said he felt he should use contemporary songs from time to time in the church services.

Mr. Hale decided to quit the choir, and he let everyone know before he left that he felt the choir director was being irreverent. His early retirement created a void in his heart, and the choir didn't seem notably worse or better without him.

"Shout with joy before the Lord, O Earth! . . . come before Him singing with joy" (Psalm 100:1, 2, LB). The choir had a problem which could not be solved by Bach, Beethoven, and bullheadedness on the one hand or "relevance," rhythm, and self-righteousness on the other. Small stuff in the heart sounds discords in the heavens.

REVIEW BOARD

A concerned group of women met together to discuss and pray for church needs. As time passed, discussion took more and more time, and prayer declined. Seemingly there were many disturbing things in the church.

For instance: "What a shame the Millers spent all that money on those sanctuary curtains. We could have gone without the curtains, but we certainly can't get through too many more weeks without more hymnbooks."

"I've really been concerned about Mr. Hare's attitude in Sunday school—he's been such a trial to the class"—the comments flowed and backtracked, always with spiritual overtones, of course. The concerns were varied: the length of someone's hair or skirt, the tastes in music or entertainment.

Somehow this group had missed Paul's directive for certain types of concern: "Steer clear of foolish discussions which lead people into the sin of anger with each other" (2 Timothy 2:16, LB).

Many debatable issues have not been made specifically right or wrong in the Scriptures. The Christian is admonished to search God's will for his own conduct and tastes, and let God decide others' behavior too.

TOUCHY SITUATION

Mrs. Anderson had slighted Mrs. Burke. At least, Mrs. Burke thought she had been slighted. "Why, she almost knocked me down and didn't say a word to me," Mrs. Burke told Mrs. Kendall.

"Come to think about it, she didn't speak to me either," sympathized Mrs. Kendall. "Maybe the Sunday school superintendent's job has gone to her head."

Quite literally it had—in the form of a terrible headache. Ten minutes before classes that particular Sunday, Mrs. Anderson was informed that two teachers were ill. To make matters worse one of the teachers had the only key to the new supply cabinet, so all the song books and flannelgraphs would be unavailable for classes that morning.

Deeply engrossed in her dilemma, Mrs. Anderson didn't see the blur or hear the voice of Mrs. Burke attempting to greet her as she rushed past. Like other Christians, Mrs. Anderson needed friends with understanding—and something more:

"Love is very patient and kind.... It is not irritable or touchy. It does not hold grudges and will hardly even notice when others do it wrong" (1 Corinthians 13:4, 5 LB).

PART THREE

'Round
and
'Round

COMMUNICATION GAP

"Oh, Harold," Susan bubbled enthusiastically to her husband on the way home from church, "our new Sunday school teacher is just fantastic. This morning we talked about . . ." and she explained in detail what had gone on in class. But Harold wasn't listening; he had a business report due early in the morning.

Susan went on and on describing the new insights she had received until they drove into their driveway, and there she realized that Harold hadn't heard a word she had said.

"I might as well not be here for all you care!" Susan scolded as she slammed the door.

After a long afternoon Susan recognized that she had not been slighted by her husband, but she had been soiled by her anger. She, not her husband, needed to seek forgiveness. Their communication broke down when she lost touch with God—even while talking about Him! How petty one can get—even on Sunday!

OFFICE STYLES

Phil Veerman walked past Don Burger's brand new desk and continued to his own office, a frown etched on his forehead and a slash on his heart.

"You know," Phil complained to his wife that evening, "I was promised a new desk over a year ago."

"Oh, I thought you did get a new desk," said Mrs. Veerman.

"A different desk, but not a new one."

"Well, how do they expect you to manage without a decent place to do your work?" asked Mrs. Veerman.

"It's not that," said Phil irritably. He didn't say immediately what "it" was that troubled him, but later it came out.

"Anybody who walked into our offices and just saw our desks would think Burger was in charge instead of me."

If desks make managers and looks guarantee reality, that might be so. But the man in charge gets and stays there by performance, not appearance. Worrying about one's prestige is a sign of losing it.

"In this new life one's nationality or race or education or social position is unimportant. Such things mean nothing; whether a person has Christ is what matters, and He is equally available to all" (Colossians 3:11, LB).

MOURNING HOURS

As an early riser, Sally is an underachiever. She simply does not enjoy starting her day with a crying, odorous baby, an adolescent who has the house in disarray because of a lost tennis shoe, or a teen-ager who either wanders around in a trancelike stupor or is a bundle of feverish activity, slamming drawers and doors to the accompaniment of blaring music.

All this can leave Sally quivering with a cup of coffee and feeling pretty ghastly. But it needn't. An S.O.S. to God when she first awakens, thanking Him for the day He has made, makes a big difference in attitude for the day.

And there are other things she could do to make morning hours more tolerable, especially on week-ends. Older children can help with the younger ones when they both insist on watching the sun come up.

Some husbands prefer to eat breakfast later in the morning, and older children can get their own breakfast if they are up early. Cold cereal, fruit juice, and toast can be readily available. The bigger breakfast can be served later—and called lunch! Books and toys that encourage quiet play for younger children can be put out the night before and help gain a few extra winks for Mother.

Mothers who don't shine at dawn should make schedules by their internal clocks and plan ahead for the rest of the family. Feeling guilty about lagging behind early risers is small potatoes. With good planning and cooperation, the family will adjust to different schedules and discover how much fun it is to be helpful and thoughtful of each other.

THE DILLINGS AND THE TRILLINGS

The Dillings and their three well-behaved young-sters live next door to the Trillings and their two incorrigible brats. At least, that's the way Mrs. Dilling looks at it.

The families were friends before Billy Trilling borrowed Rollie Dilling's bicycle and returned it with a bent rear wheel. When questioned, Billy insisted the wheel was that way when he took the bike. Though Rollie admits he has left his bike lying in the drive-way off and on for weeks, he is sure it was in perfect working condition when Billy borrowed it.

Both mothers steadfastly defend their sons' opin-ions and refuse to let them play together. And the women are no longer speaking to each other, of course.

The Dillings had the bike repaired and sent the bill to the Trillings. The Trillings returned the bill with a note saying they were not responsible for the damage and did not intend to be goaded into paying for Rollie's habitual carelessness just because Billy had the misfortune to use the bike just before the damage was discovered.

Communications between the two families are now all written impersonally. The sight of a member of the enemy camp causes the combatants to take circuitous routes to avoid confrontation. One trembles to imagine the fireworks on that day when a wayward baseball lands in the foreign yard or crashes a window pane!

How small can we get? Would not the $3.98 cost of a new wheel be a big investment in friendship and neighborhood harmony? True charity would direct both families to offer to pay, but if neither family can stir up such charity they will suffer numerous other bent and broken things. "Stop being mean, bad-tempered, and angry. Quarreling, harsh words, and dislike of others should have no place in your lives. Instead, be kind to each other, tenderhearted, forgiving one another, just as God has forgiven you because you belong to Christ" (Ephesians 4:31, 32, LB).

BIG OPERATOR

A visit to Mrs. Trent's is a painful experience. Upon arrival, you are inundated by half-finished work: a living room bulging with a vacuum cleaner, basket of laundry on its way somewhere, a stack of empty boxes—Mrs. Trent's "cleaning" is "in progress."

Unfortunately, Mrs. Trent is breathing heavily in a stuffed chair, scrub brush in hand, regaining her strength for another task. We have interrupted her afternoon work—scrubbing the siding on the outside of her house. Had we arrived this morning, we might have disturbed her monumental effort to file hundreds of recipes that look like something she might want to try sometime.

Mrs. Trent is tired. In fact, she's exhausted. She has worked hard, but all around her is more work to be done. Her floor is dirty, her beds unmade, and she asks for *our* suggestions as to what to serve for

107

dinner. Worst of all, her family doesn't appreciate her toil, she says.

A look around the house inclines the visitor to sympathize with the family. Mrs. Trent has lost sight of her real job. Though she works hard, she is not caring for the immediate needs of her family. Instead of filing recipes she should be organizing today's dinner and doing this morning's dishes. She should scrub her kitchen floor and let the rain or her husband take care of the outside of the house. She is majoring in minors.

Mrs. Trent needs to re-evaluate her priorities and put "family" instead of "projects" high on her list. Perhaps all she can accomplish on a daily basis will be beds made, rooms straightened, meals on time, clothes properly cared for. Those big projects are small stuff which distract her from primary responsibilities. "She watches carefully all that goes on throughout her household. . . . Her children stand and bless her; so does her husband" (Proverbs 31:27, 28, LB).

MORE THAN HALFWAY

"Sometimes," remarked Mr. Garrett wistfully, "I think you don't love me at all."

His young wife snapped with righteous fury: "Look at me! I'm a mess. Work, work, work, all day long! The house, the baby, and a job besides!"

"But I just wanted you to sit here and talk for a minute," suggested her husband weakly.

"That's all very well for those who have *time* to sit and don't have to cook supper and do dishes and pick up clothes—" And another evening of hot words and oppressive atmosphere closed in on the Garetts.

How sad—and unnecessary—for a couple who vowed to love each other "till death do us part." In the accumulating demands of marriage and a family they forgot why they began the venture!

Each partner's being willing to "go halfway" to make the marriage successful is not the answer. It wasn't enough for winning a mate and it's not enough

111

to keep one. Love, self-sacrificing love, is the only good answer.

God is the source of this kind of love. "We know how dearly God loves us, and we feel this warm love everywhere within us because God has given us the Holy Spirit to fill our hearts with His love" (Romans 5:5, LB).

Feuds over who is the *most* tired or most over-worked is "small stuff." The question is not who needs help the most, but who will obey God in being kind and tenderhearted.

A big first step is to read together 1 Corinthians 13:4-7 and rediscover the characteristics of love. Then prayer for reconciling love will be answered, for it is surely according to God's will.

After you're assured that the love of God again rules your home, undertake some planning to coordinate the compressed schedules and activities to everyone's advantage. No family can eliminate every strain, but by seeing love prevail in the small stuff, we can sincerely say, "This is the day the Lord has made. We will rejoice and be glad in it." (Psalm 118:24).